Each of Us
Is a Book

Each of Us Is a Book

Poems for the Library Minded

by DAVID DRAKE

McFarland & Company, Inc., Publishers
Jefferson, North Carolina, and London

Library of Congress Cataloguing-in-Publication Data

Drake, David, 1949–
    Each of us is a book : poems for the library minded /
by David Drake.
       p.   cm.

    ISBN 0-7864-1568-1 (softcover : 50# alkaline paper) ∞

    1. Libraries—Poetry.   2. Library science—Poetry.
3. Books and reading—Poetry.   I. Title.
PS3554.R19615E15 2003
811'.54—dc21
                                2002156685

British Library cataloguing data are available

Cover photograph ©2003 PhotoDisc

Manufactured in the United States of America

*McFarland & Company, Inc., Publishers
  Box 611, Jefferson, North Carolina 28640
   www.mcfarlandpub.com*

In loving memory of my grandmother,
May Nelson Kelly, 1910–2000

Genesis 31:49

Contents

LIBRARIANS / CYBRARIANS

THE READING LIFE

Our Patrons, Ourselves

The Writing Life

TOOLS OF THE TRADE

Preface

Does anyone read prefaces? I usually don't, so I am in the position of having to write something I wouldn't care to read, which is even worse than having to read something I wouldn't care to write, although anyone who has been a librarian for awhile has done plenty of both. Think of all the memos, annual reports, grant proposals, and other tortured prose we are forced to produce and consume. Better yet, don't think of them. This is a book of poetry, and those documents are the antithesis of all things poetic.

The purpose of a preface, as I see it, is threefold: to give prospective readers the book's intended scope; to provide some background on its development; and to convince the wavering that they really do want to read it. I'm not sure I can accomplish even one of those three (and one hit out of three swings would be considered excellent in baseball, but not in the literary world). But I'll try.

These poems are for the library minded, which is of course mostly librarians but could include, and I hope would include, readers other than librarians. Not that there's anything wrong with having librarians as your target audience. I know of no other group I would rather be read by than my peers. Following the publication of my first book of library poetry, *Overdue Notice*, I received many nice letters and e-mails which continue even today. Poems from that 1995 book have been read at new library dedications and other formal occasions; quoted in articles, newsletters, and websites; printed on calendars; posted on staff bulletin boards; and presented in any number of other ways

1

I never would have expected. One reader even gave me credit for inspiring her to attend library school! I am flattered and touched by this attention, particularly since my primary goal in writing *Overdue Notice* was to create poems that working librarians could relate to and enjoy. I have the same goal for *Each of Us Is a Book*, and if a few non-librarians enjoy it, too, so much the better.

Like its predecessor, this book grew out of my desire to poeticize the things and personages of our library world. It hasn't been all that hard. I have found libraries to be full of poetic moments, almost all of them unintentional and unexpected. As in candid photographs, the framing of a seemingly mundane activity in a poem often reveals qualities we never notice in the larger context. Or so I would hope. I've never pretended that my poems were anything more than little amusements or opportunities for evanescent reflection. If I have taken any pride in them, it is because they deal with themes and topics that are not covered by anyone else but are, in my opinion at least, worthy of notice.

So there, briefly, are the scope, background, and sales pitch. Everything else is left to you, the reader. I've done my part. I hope these poems make some connection to your inner library, whatever your outer connection to libraries may be.

ARENAS OF POSSIBILITY

"The library is an arena of possibility,
opening both a window into the soul
and a door onto the world."
—*Rita Dove*

Book Sale

We sell books so we can buy more.
Books, that is.
We sell our worn-out books.
Duplicates, donated duds.
Books we don't want.
Old books, odd books.
Somebody may want them.
Somebody usually does.
You never know why.
Not always for reading.
One year, a guy bought stacks of paperbacks.
He buried them in his garden.
Filled in the low spots.
He said it worked well.
Kept the soil from washing.
I didn't know you could do that.
Interior decorators buy our books.
To fill shelves, for looks.
They don't care what the books are.
Just so they look good.
But most people buy them because they're cheap.
And because buying a book makes you feel smart.
Buying a cheap book makes you feel smarter.
You got a bargain.
Even if you never read it.
Which most never do, I'm convinced.
The books end up in garage sales.
Or back in our sale.
That's OK.
We sell books so we can buy more.
Let it continue.

Bookmobile, 1960

They didn't have a branch library
in our part of Dallas then,
but that didn't matter so much
once the bookmobile started coming.
They parked it in one of the lots
of the Casa View Shopping Center,
a double strip of storefronts
that sprawled a quarter-mile
down the urban prairie.

I'd never seen anything to match it
in all my eleven years:
it wasn't a building, it wasn't a car,
but a strange hybrid of both,
a corpulent steel beast
with books in its belly,
a friendly beast who welcomed all
into that belly to share the bounty.

So in I would go,
into the belly of the friendly fat beast
that hummed and vibrated as it rested
in the parking lot on Tuesday nights.
The feeble lighting flickered
and the air conditioning hissed wearily
as it tried with little success
to drive out the sultry summer air,
but none of that lessened the allure
of what waited inside.

And I was so thrilled
to browse the bookshelves
that flanked the narrow aisle
where two could scarcely walk abreast.
I didn't mind the line was long,
or the press of bodies so great
elbows and heads had frequent encounters;
I clutched the library card my mother signed
and selected with sheer joy
the three books allowed to me.

I remember some of those books still:
Circus Doctor, a veterinarian's story
of life under the big top —
I kept renewing that one
because I liked it so well;
Treasure Island, Stevenson's classic tale
of pirates and adventure, told by a boy;
and *David Balfour*, because Stevenson wrote it, too.
It wasn't as good as *Treasure Island*,
but it was about a boy who, like me,
was named David, and I loved seeing my name
in big letters on the cover of a book.

That was such a long time ago,
but there are still bookmobiles out there,
a few scattered somewhere, filled with books,
and there are still eleven-year-olds
who may know that same joy I knew.
Do they?
I hope they do, I truly hope so.

Brown

There was a very old library
I visited once years ago, briefly,
and everything I recall of it
is in shades of brown: the walls,
the floors, the furniture, the books,
even the clothes of the people
who worked there in the brown light.

My memory of that library remains
for no good reason I can grasp
other than its odd monochrome aspect;
one of those things you just remember
as if your mind had to plug a hole
and that was all that was around
to push into the void.

Don't Bank on It

If banks were keen on service
And cared about us, too,
They'd open nights and weekends
The way libraries do.

Familiar Sounds

Familiar sounds...
the background music
of our workday:

the faint beeps of barcodes being read

indistinct conversations

clattering keyboards

books being slapped shut

the squeaking wheels of overloaded book trucks

mothers shushing children

children *not* shushed by their mothers

the whispered hum of the laser printer

laughter, too loud, quickly stifled

books dropping down the return chute

pulsating repetitions of the photocopier:
phutt-phutt-phutt-phutt

something metallic dropped, bouncing

you-know-who complaining

Famous First Lines

Wherein the author asserts his poetic license
to revise slightly the openings
of some well-known poems,
that they may have a library slant.

Once upon a midnight dreary, while I pondered, weak and weary,
My computer screen grew bleary from a late-night reference query.
    Edgar Allan Poe
    "The Raven"

When I was one-and-twenty,
I owed the library plenty.
My fines accumulated
'Cause I procrastinated.
    A.E. Housman
    A Shropshire Lad, XIII

A Book of Verses underneath the Bough
Was stolen from the library just now.
    Omar Khayyam
    The Rubaiyat, 12

Listen, my children, and you shall hear
A worn-out cassette that's not too clear.
    Henry Wadsworth Longfellow
    "Paul Revere's Ride"

I think that I shall never see
New carpet in this library.
The concrete shows through every thread
Like skin upon a balding head.
    Joyce Kilmer
    "Trees"

A thing of beauty is a joy for ever:
A problem patron leaves us never.
    John Keats
    "Endymion"

The curfew tolls the knell of parting day,
Yet still our patrons will not go away.
They linger by the desk and in their chairs;
I've told them we are closing — no one cares.
    Thomas Gray
    "Elegy (Written in a Country Churchyard)"

Out of the night that covers me,
(We've lost our electricity)
I grope around to guide myself,
And bang my knee against a shelf.
    William Ernest Henley
    "Invictus"

Let us go then, you and I
Through the stacks until we spy
This call number on this book,
Pull it off and take a look.
    T.S. Eliot
    "The Love Song of J. Alfred Prufrock"

I should like to rise and go
But the boss said no, and so
I'll remain here cataloging,
Fantasizing of his flogging.
    Robert Louis Stevenson
    "Travel"

Blessings on thee, little man,
Please be quiet, if you can!
Take this book and try to read it.
Is it break time? Oh, I need it!
    John Greenleaf Whittier
    "The Barefoot Boy"

'Twas brillig, and the slithy toves
Were reading in the north alcoves.
    Lewis Carroll
    "Jabberwocky"

I wandered lonely as a cloud
(Those fourth-floor stacks don't draw a crowd.)
    William Wordsworth
    "The Daffodils"

Who is Sylvia, what is she,
This reference question you bring me?
Sylvia Plath? Is that her, please?
She's shelved right there among the P's.
    William Shakespeare
    "Who Is Sylvia?"

Something there is that doesn't love a wall,
Especially in restrooms; after all,
Our restroom walls were once so clean and bright,
But they're unloved, so on them people write.
    Robert Frost
    "Mending Walls"

My heart leaps up when I behold
My search brought hits a thousandfold.
    William Wordsworth
    "My Heart Leaps Up When I Behold"

Hail to thee, blithe spirit!
Your radio—I hear it,
As all do, I presume,
Here in the reading room.
I'll tell you just once more:
Please turn the volume lower.
    Percy Bysshe Shelley
    "To a Skylark"

The Library A to Z

(for younger readers, and those still young at heart)

A is for an **Almanac,**
With facts and figures we need;

B is for **Books** (of course!),
From cover to cover to read;

C is for the **Catalog,**
The way that we find a book;

D is for **Dewey Decimal System,**
The numbers tell us where to look;

E is for **Electronic,**
Technology brings us so much;

F is for **Full Text,**
Magazines, books, and such;

G is for **Gazetteer,**
Geography, names, and places;

H is for all our **Holdings,**
The stuff that's throughout these spaces;

I is for the **Internet,**
That brings the whole world to your screen;

J is for **Journal,**
A scholarly magazine;

K is for **Keyword,**
A way for a search to start;

L is for **Librarians,**
Who are so helpful and smart;

M is for **Microfilm** (or -fiche),
With words that are microscopic;

N is for **Newspaper,**
With news on every topic;

O is for **Overdue,**
Sometimes we get a reminder;

P is for **Periodical,**
Sometimes they go to the binder;

Q is for **Quiet,**
We can talk, but please don't shout;

R is for **Reference,**
Helpful books that don't check out;

S is for **Subjects,**
The names of the things we seek;

T is for **Thesaurus,**
For help as we write or we speak;

U is for **URL,**
An address on the Internet;

V is for **Volumes,**
When there's more than one book in a set;

W is for **World Wide Web,**
All those web pages we see;

X is for **Xerox**
(Really, what else could it be?);

Y is for **Yearbook,**
For that year, what came to pass;

Z is for **Zeroes,**
The first Dewey Decimal class!

Library America

There are three towns
in the United States
named Reading:
Reading, Illinois.
Reading, Ohio.
Reading, Pennsylvania.
Yes, I know
the one in PA
is pronounced "redding,"
but that's their problem.
California's got a Redding,
and *they* know how to spell it.
As far as I know,
the other two Readings
are pronounced as they should
  be,
like *reading* a book.
And there is also
Readstown, Wisconsin.
Are people reading in Reading
while everybody reads in Reads-
  town?

Do you know
Weed, California?
I've been there.
It's a lovely little town
in the shadow
of Mount Shasta.
Does the library in Weed weed?
Of course it does,
and if I helped,
we'd weed in Weed
while they're reading in Reading.

And what about
Magazine Mountain, Arkansas?
Oh, I'll bet
they named it that
because they kept ammunition
there,
but so what?
Wouldn't it be
a great location
for a subscription agency?

Someday I'll visit
Booker, Texas,
just because
I like the name.
They have a high school.
I wondered what
their mascot is,
so I checked.
They're the Kiowas.
I'm disappointed.
I was hoping
they might be
the Librarians.

Library Limericks

Author's Note: The limerick is the only fixed poetic form indigenous to the English language. It is also considered rather lowbrow by scholars. For both these reasons, I like it!

1

Mel Dewey endured the frustration
Of books with no organization,
Until from his perch
One morning in church
He got a 10-point revelation.

2

A cataloger known as Miss Jane
One day went completely insane
And chose to erase
Her entire database,
Shouting, "Mistress of my own domain!"

3

A reference librarian named Nate
Proceeded at such a slow rate
When patrons approached him,
He always reproached them
To just take a number and wait.

4

A library page known as Dwight
Dispensed with call numbers outright,
Deciding one day
To shelve books his way:
By color, by thickness, and height.

5

A city librarian named Bob
Found politics made his heart throb
Until he did err
Upstaging the mayor
And found himself out of a job.

6

A library clerk known as Ned
Doused the lights and used candles instead.
When asked to explain,
With utter disdain,
"Ambiance!" was all that he said.

7

A serials librarian named Tate
For marriage no longer could wait
And so filed a claim
For a wife in his name,
Since it worked when the journals were late.

8

Although the staff lounge is a mess,
Nobody will ever confess
To making it so,
And so we all know
It will stay a pigsty, more or less.

9

The plants in our library died
Though Herb, our director, had tried
To keep them all growing,
Postmortems were showing
They all died from pure Herbicide.

10

A book is a loveable item:
Some love to read 'em, and some love to write 'em.
When loaned and returned,
Libraries have learned
That babies and dogs love to bite 'em.

11

For Reference, Jean has a flair;
She sits with a smile in her chair
And answers all day,
"The bathroom's that way,"
But says it with such *savoir faire.*

12

I toil in a wondrous profession,
But I have to make a confession:
If I had it over,
I'd be a sheep drover —
The better to vent my aggression.

13

A library patron named Hope
Was always a true misanthrope.
She cherished her books
But gave dirty looks
To everyone, even the Pope.

14

When seeking a rhyme for "library,"
Alternatives simply are scary.
This limerick craft
Can make one quite daft,
Ill-tempered, confused, and contrary.

15

Our evening librarian, Kate,
Believes we are open too late.
She shows for her duties
In nightgown and booties
And lies on the carpet prostrate.

16

A circ clerk with great agitation
Departed this world at his station.
The doctor who said
The fellow was dead
Ascribed it to poor circulation.

17

We host a perpetual vagrant
Whose hygienic lapses are flagrant.
He sits in a chair
All day over there
And smells something far less than fragrant.

18

Jane's stuck in the staff elevator
And someone should go extricate her,
But first let us take
A long coffee break,
Because of the way we all hate her.

19

Today in his obituary
They said that he ran the library,
But never a word
Of how death occurred
(The wife and the new secretary.)

20

It's always a bee in my bonnet —
This paycheck with my name upon it
Confirms what they say
Of library pay:
No one but a monk could live on it!

21

Most times I'm a quite normal fella,
But sometimes I grab an umbrella
And run through the stacks
And try to relax
By dancing a fast tarantella.

22

A library boss brash and bold
Who bragged that "his girls" did as told
Was gone from the place
One day with no trace.
(That basement is so dark and cold.)

23

Our college library is praised,
But whenever money is raised,
It all seems to go
To football, and so
If we get a cent, I'm amazed!

24

Camilla unlocked all the doors
And saw the footprints on the floors,
But then stared agog
At the card catalog
And shouted, *"Who's been in my drawers?"*

25

An avid young reader named Gary
Read through the entire dictionary.
They called him a nerd,
But with every word,
Did he get much smarter? Yes, very.

26

That vendor drops by twice a year,
Not calling before he comes here,
But I have a hunch
He'll pay for my lunch,
And therefore, my schedule is clear.

27

Big Bertha is such a great reader —
Oh, none in this world can exceed her!
We should give her honor,
Pin ribbons upon her,
But then, of course, we'd have to feed her.

28

Big Bertha, in tones that were curt,
Complained that all over she hurt.
She felt all around
And finally found
Ten books in the folds of her skirt.

29

That couch in the big reading room:
I knew it would soon meet its doom
When Bertha placed there
Her grand derriere —
It promptly collapsed with a boom!

30

Big Bertha had marvelous diction
And read with impressive conviction
Till one day she fell,
Rolled down the stairwell,
And came to a halt in the Fiction.

31

A bibliophile known as Brooke
On top of her head glued a book.
Though people would stare,
She just didn't care,
And said, "You don't like it? Don't look."

32

The source of my library career?
The memory is ever so clear:
I couldn't do math,
So this was my path
Instead of an engineer.

33

The library at the North Pole
Sometimes can get out of control.
The library elves
Climb up on the shelves
And dive in the big wassail bowl.

34

That patron is beyond belief!
She causes us nothing but grief.
When she's out the door,
We dance round the floor
And all breathe a sigh of relief.

35

Our children's librarian, Sunny,
Is known to be witty and funny.
Each time someone asks
Why she does her tasks,
She says she's just in for the money.

36

Our reference librarian, Tess,
Wears overalls— never a dress.
She looks so agrarian,
A rustic librarian;
For fashion she couldn't care less.

37

A library in North Carolina
Had perched by its entrance a mynah,
Till one day the bird
Repeated *that* word —
He's now in a zoo back in China.

38

Our patrons ignored overdues
Until we decided to use
A wiseguy named Jack,
Who gets our books back
With offers no one can refuse.

39

I learned it in library school:
A reference book is a tool,
Like drills and chainsaws,
But better because
It doesn't make noise or use fuel.

40

Our ILL librarian, old Joan,
Just loves to complain, gripe, and moan.
There's no use pretending,
We wish we were sending
Her on interlibrary loan!

41

Librarians don't like to fuss,
But public perception of us
And all that we do
Is so far from true,
I just want to holler and cuss!

42

Our favorite patron, old Fred,
Drapes newspapers over his head
And sleeps by the door —
If he doesn't snore,
We check him to see if he's dead.

43

Librarians are often like wine:
With age, some grow ever more fine,
And others more sour
With each passing hour.
Your library has them, and mine.

44

A large, angry patron in Dallas
Reacted with words of such malice
To fines we applied
That we fled outside,
Afraid that he might disembowel us!

45

A library professor named Trevor,
Who thought himself learned and clever,
Concealed with great prudence
The fact from his students
He'd not worked in a library, ever.

46

Our magazines sit on display,
Consistent in every way:
Celebrity covers,
Suggestions for lovers,
And topics most trendy today.

47

A library patron named Hugh
Had two books due he forgot to renew.
He, Hugh, had no clue;
And all of us who
Knew Hugh knew, too, Hugh knew not they were due.

48

A catalog clerk known as Mabel
Became so proficient and able
She rose to great fame
And multitudes came
To watch her affix a spine label.

49

A reference fellow named Ewing
Ate snacks over books he was viewing.
The books got all stained
And patrons complained,
But Ewing just kept right on chewing.

50

A library poet named Drake
Scrawls rhymes that sometimes make one ache,
And often his verse
From bad goes to worse;
Be patient, and give him a break!

The Library of Lost Books

All lost library books
belong to only one library:
The Library of Lost Books.
It is a vast and diverse library;
no one knows its numbers
or its locations,
yet it is as real
as any library within walls,
for a library is defined
least of all by walls.
The Library of Lost Books
is the patchwork shadow, the reverse image
of all working libraries everywhere.
It cannot be visited, or even found.
It has no staff, no patrons, no funding.
But it grows, it spreads.
The diaspora continues.

Library Proverbs

Great books make great readers.

A grinning vendor has much to hide.

Large computer problems are always smaller than they seem; small computer problems are always larger than they seem.

A book in the hand is worth two on order.

Catalogers start with much information and narrow it; reference librarians start with little information and expand it.

A question unasked is a door unopened.

Computers and children grow constantly in memory.

A true story that is never read is no less true.

The ultimate binary code is "dead or alive."

A library of a million books must be read one at a time.

The best answers raise more questions.

Librarians should be guides, not gurus.

Biography is a statue sculpted with words.

Voluntary ignorance costs dearly.

A hastily written memo will always be regretted.

Without the binding, the book falls apart; without a book, the binding is useless.

A blind man can read in the dark.

The missing volume contains the answer.

A book torn in half is not two books.

Strive for few words and much information.

Ink is to paper what blood is to the body.

Every censor has his own secret.

Culture is the storehouse of humanity. Libraries are the storehouses of culture.

Ignorance cannot perceive itself.

Literacy is the passport to knowledge.

A book banned is never forgotten.

Library Senryu

Author's Note: most readers are familiar with haiku, the seventeen-syllable miniature poems of Japanese origin that seek to capture moments of heightened awareness in simple language and follow the form of three lines with 5, 7, and 5 syllables respectively. A true haiku must deal with themes of nature and each poem traditionally refers to a season. Senryu, which follows the same 5-7-5 form, deals instead with human situations, often humorous or satirical, and seems to me particularly suited to the library.

1

some books are missing
from the shelf that sags deeply
a gap-toothed smile

2

she waits for a ride
the library is closing
outside, it's raining

3

a red baseball cap
and yesterday's newspaper
the old man dozes

4

light through a window
dust sparkles in little clouds
and lands on the books

5

our new computers
all hum in sweet unison
can we dance to it?

6

cleaning the carpet
behind the file cabinet
so many dead bugs

7

children encircle
a smiling librarian
the story hour starts

8

inside the drawer
an old newspaper clipping
brown at the edges

9

lights flicker and fade
the power is out again
we sit in darkness

10

bronze plaque on the wall
tells who built the library
nobody reads it

11

afternoon before
a long holiday weekend
the staff grows restless

12

somebody's kitten
got into the library
where is it hiding?

13

patron is angry
says she returned her late books
we know she didn't

14

left on a table
a child's red woolen mitten
somewhere, a cold hand

15

our new director
first day at the library
we watch her closely

16

brisk wind blows papers
someone left the door open
get up and shut it

17

heads bent to books
all around the reading room
swans poised on a pond

18

this memorandum
I don't know what he's saying
I've read it three times

19

big stuffed animals
in the children's department
kids play hide-and-seek

20

I just can't believe
it's still at the bindery
maybe they lost it

21

these books on the shelves
turn their backs as if to say
read me, I dare you

22

junk mail in big piles
on my desk each afternoon
call me a junkman

23

there in the lobby
that guy we threw out last night
well — he's back again

24

laughter is constant
drifting from the meeting room
something is funny

25

that water fountain
watch out when you drink from it
blasts you in the face

26

library is closed
I've told her twice already
but she just won't leave

27

we have fresh doughnuts
at our monthly staff meetings
I like maple best

28

the screen goes crazy
when you hit Enter
see, I told you so

29

tiny little girl
stands before the display case
staring intently

30

boxes of new books
colors of a flowerbed
jackets slick and crisp

31

those fluorescent lights
keep flickering on and off
disco library

32

we still get bulk mail
addressed to staff who retired
some are even dead

33

she's never left home
but loves to read travel books
a wandering mind

34

that statue outside
the pigeons really love it
time to hose it down

35

the mayor is bragging
about our new library
he's never been there

36

open on a stand
unabridged dictionary
a sprawling giant

37

sound of books falling
an avalanche in the stacks
I'm afraid to look

38

Christmas exhibit
still in the big display case
late January

39

patron talks non-stop
librarian is smiling
her thoughts are elsewhere

40

we turn the lights off
voices shout from the darkness
they haven't left yet

41

they meet on Tuesdays
our Friends of the Library
some are not friendly

42

twenty-three years old
Young Adult Librarian
the title suits her

43

unusual books
and unusual people
are found together

44

I thought I would laugh
as my retirement drew near
instead I am sad

45

when she brings books back
they always smell like lemons
what's going on there?

46

so very quiet
dark and empty library
little sounds leap out

47

Dewey Decimal
the best system, period!
no pun intended

48

a true book lover
will even read the preface
well, sometimes at least

49

in library school
they don't tell you about this—
what a day I've had!

50

old card catalogs
sometimes you waited your turn
to search through a tray

Misconceptions

Abstract: specialized exercise equipment for the midsection
AGRICOLA: what farmers drink
ANSI: nervous or impatient
Branch manager: horticulturist
Controlled vocabulary: a violation of the First Amendment
Digital preservation: using a good hand cream
Domain: food poisoning
el-hi: mass transit in Chicago
Fascicle: a frozen treat enjoyed by Mussolini
Homepage: a library assistant in the 'hood
Microforms: bacteria
Modem: to top desserts with ice cream
Retrocon: an elderly prison inmate
Serial port: cheap wine made from grain
Statement of responsibility: a confession
Stop list: something police carry
UNIX: neutered men

National Library Week

It's National Library Week — let's have a party!
Forget the posters, displays, and events.
Do you think any of our patrons
really care about them anyway?
If they notice at all,
they think it's nice we have a week
to recognize libraries. How quaint.
The librarians have their own week.
Then they forget all about it.
So let's celebrate by having a party,
a party for *us,* and forget the expense.
It's only once a year.
Let's have a party!

Nobody

If you've been in an academic library
late on a Friday afternoon,
you know how empty it can be.
Students and faculty are mostly not there,
having started their weekend,
leaving the library staff largely alone.
At one such library years ago,
I was director and had as my boss
a vice-president, a tiny little man
whose mind matched his physical stature.
On Friday afternoons he walked around the campus,
dropping into offices, ostensibly to visit
but really to see if anyone left early.
In the library we never, ever left early
but he always came around anyway,
peeking into workspaces, greeting staff
whose names he never learned
with the strained and painful smile
of the natural pessimist.
Then, he would gaze across the open floor
and wonder aloud where all the students were.
Otherwise, we never saw the man.
He was never there in the mornings
when the floor was teeming with activity,
or when long lines formed
at the busy circulation desk,
or when we instructed hordes of freshmen
in the mysteries of the library;
yet whenever he and I met in his office,
he always told me it concerned him
that nobody came to the library.
He was right, I suppose;
he was nobody, and he came to the library.

Old Libraries

New libraries are all very well
with their clean lines and ample glass,
but old libraries have a quality,
as was often said of old movie stars.
Not quality as in worth,
though they have that, too—
a quality, that *je ne sais quoi*
which in libraries comes only with age.

I love to walk in the wake
of countless thousands before me
who also trod the creaking floors
amid the plaster walls and dark wood,
inhaling that marvelous scent,
the odd yet sweet fragrance
that comes of blending books, a building,
and memories.

When I am an old man,
I want to sit all day
in an old chair in an old library
and read an old book;
dozing perhaps, rising at times
to meander through narrow stacks
and browse the overstuffed shelves,
reliving the serendipitous joys of my youth.

Build the new libraries, yes,
in the centers of communities everywhere,
build them for our children, and theirs.
Just leave a few old libraries around.
They aren't sleek or dynamic,
but they have that quality that deserves saving.
Like older people, they still have much to share
if we're not too quick to dismiss them.

The Perfect Library

Some day we may see
The perfect library,
But it seems to me
We should be quite wary
Of claiming perfection
For any one yet —
Who knows, on reflection,
How good we can get?

Perfection

Our library is quiet, untroubled, serene;
The shelves are in order, exact and pristine;
The tables and chairs are aligned, straight and formal;
But soon we will open and get back to normal.

plink, plink

an old piano
someone donated long ago
sits in the meeting room
all day long plink, plink

because our director
couldn't say no
it sits in the meeting room
all day long plink, plink

so many people
go in the meeting room
and pound on the piano
all day long plink, plink

most of them can't
play the piano one lick
but still pound the keys
all day long plink, plink

grownups or kids
it doesn't matter
they pound on the keys
all day long plink, plink

our director refuses
to lock the meeting room
bad public relations
all day long plink, plink

I'm having nightmares
that piano laughs at me
its keys are like teeth
all night long plink, plink

I'm going to steal it
in the middle of night
load in on an old truck
and rattle away plink, plink

to the edge of a canyon
I'll push it over
and hear when it crashes
one final gasp plink, plink

Presidential Libraries

They are really not libraries at all,
but archives and museums;
yet as the single highest tribute
to our highest elected officials,
the leaders of our nation,
they are called libraries;
and by so honoring our presidents,
we honor our libraries.

The Pub

Whenever anyone refers to a "pub"
they of course mean a tavern,
since "pub" is short for "public bar,"
which is what they call them in Britain,
where both terms originated.

But in America, at least,
why can't we use "pub"
to mean a public library?
As in, "I'm going down to the pub
for a quick novel. Don't wait up."

We could even get dartboards...

Rules

Most libraries, at least I think,
Have rules forbidding food and drink;
Most have a rule regarding quiet;
At any rate, we all go by it.

It's not that we're opposed to fun;
We like it much as anyone.
We say eat, drink, and be merry —
Just not here in our library!

Tornado

They don't teach about tornadoes in library school,
but in Texas we grow up with twisters
and know what to do when they come.
We knew what to do that spring day
when the afternoon sky grew suddenly dark
and the warning sirens raised their fierce wails.

Our library had a basement, a big one.
We gathered down there, staff and patrons,
to wait it out. Everybody was calm.
Some of the young men told jokes
to show they were bold and unafraid;
one even pretended he wanted to go upstairs,
outside, to watch the approach of the storm.
We wouldn't let him. He barely objected.

Everyone else waited with stoic patience,
chatting quietly or sitting with arms folded.
Our library was no longer a library.
It was a shelter, a haven.
We waited.
The whirling winds grew louder,
louder, then faded into silence.

Cautiously, a few of us went upstairs.
We were lucky.
It had been a weak tornado;
its outer edge only brushed us.
Debris in rough disarray littered the campus
and we lost two big trees,
but the library and other buildings were unharmed.
Nobody was hurt.
It was a time for celebration, for relief.

I didn't tell anyone, but in the basement
I'd had visions of the library bursting open,
all our books drawn upward into the spiral
to be hurled from the sky miles away,
ripped apart, pages fluttering down like birds.
It never happened, and I'm still glad.

Upstaged

The kids' department bought
A brand-new red computer.
It's cute, but to my thought
The kids are so much cuter.

What's New?

Some libraries tend to greet
Innovation with suspicion
Until it grows obsolete —
Then they hail it as tradition.

When the Line
Snakes Round the Corner

When the line snakes round the corner
as they wait for us to open;
when we're here twenty-four hours
to accommodate the crush;
when attendance grows to rival
that in stadiums of sport;
when we build in wild expansion
to make room for all our patrons;
when the money flows so freely
that we bask in fat abundance;
when the televisions darken
as their owners seek us first;
when libraries are respected
as the power halls of learning;
when librarians are courted
as purveyors of the magic;
when these fantasies turn truthful,
we will know we have arrived.

LIBRARIANS / CYBRARIANS

Aspiring to Be
a Library Director?

Aspiring to be a Library Director?
Whom cynical types would perceive a defector,
A sellout with motives mired deeply in malice,
A stone-hearted misanthrope, evil and callous?

I've been one for years, so these secrets I'm sharing:
They send us to school so we're brusque and uncaring.
We're trained to ignore your sound, well-reasoned planning
While small acts we see as insurgence we're banning.

We turn a blind eye to your pitiful pleading
As we pronounce dictums ill-thought and misleading.
We practice for hours to be prejudicial
And never let logic reverse what's official.

So carefully choose the pathway you would follow —
If your head and heart are both tiny and hollow,
You might make a Director, so give it a try;
But if you're bright and caring, you need not apply.

At Your Service

When I'm working the reference desk
The patrons I'm constantly meeting
May think I'm somewhat picaresque
When I give them my usual greeting.
As they come to my tiny enclave,
I smile at them and I will say,
"Good morning, my name is Dave —
I'll be your librarian today!"

Backwards

I may be the only one,
But it seems peculiar to me
That when we have just begun
We're granted our "master's" degree!

Bad Morning

While I'm at work,
I'm thinking about my break.
While I'm on break,
I'm thinking about my work.

Beautiful Dreamer

Bob's asleep, head on his desk,
Dreaming dreams so picturesque?
No one knows, but he is snoring
Loud enough to shake the flooring.

On his desk, saliva pooling
From the stream that he is drooling;
Necktie hanging loose and flapping,
Blown by snores as he sprawls napping.

Every day at half-past two
This routine begins anew;
Still, it's not a total loss—
We nap, too, 'cause he's the boss!

Before It Was

Before it was a library, it was only a building,
empty, a shell. Painted and carpeted,
but still just a space to be filled in some way.
I remember how we put the first shelf together,
got it wrong, and had to start over —
we weren't handy, we were just librarians.

We labored with a purpose: we were making a library
where one had never been. Clad in jeans and old shirts,
we pondered our every task, however small,
as if we were raising a majestic cathedral,
and to us it was indeed a holy place of sorts.
We were so young, so unjaded.

Some work a lifetime and never get to do this.
Some have the chance and forfeit it,
though I can't imagine why.
We thought it a privilege, even a mission,
to prepare the place for those who would come
in the weeks, months, years, decades ahead.

Would we ever again find so much joy
in what most would see as drudgery?
I'd like to think I'd do it now as gladly,
looking back twenty-five years,
remembering the moments like random trinkets
strung together in a child's necklace:

We sat on the floor eating sandwiches,
ringed by boxes and boxes of bright new books.
Books with fresh labels and stiff pockets,
motley-clad soldiers reporting for duty.
And we shelved them like soldiers, thousands in order,
row on row, column on column, standing at attention.

Red-faced and laughing, we dragged furniture across the floor
and argued where it should go. Afternoons passed
as the library-to-be grew around us. When we finished,
we knew that wistful satisfaction of the workman
who leaves something of himself in his craft.
We lingered a long while before leaving.

Beyond the blur of opening day and the dedication,
when so many others appeared for their first and only time
to modestly take credit for generalized glories,
beyond the years and countless parades of strangers,
we can still claim the memory of those few days
for those few who were there.

I haven't been there for a long, long time.
All the people from back then are gone now,
far gone, to other places, other libraries.
The last time I was there, I told a clerk,
"I helped put this library together before it opened."
She smiled indulgently but didn't say anything.

And why should she? It was no great thing,
only a pleasant little episode, a footnote
in the history of one little library,
a scrapbook memory for a few aging librarians,
the only ones who can truly remember
before it was a library, it was only a building.

Beginner's Lament

No one pays attention
To my suggestions.
I've got all the answers—
They don't ask the questions.

In library school
I learned how to do it,
But now that I'm here,
They won't listen to it.

Bored on the Reference Desk

I'm bored on the reference desk,
time drags by.
Surf the Web until I'm blind.
Bend a paper clip.
Read a magazine.
Get a drink of water.
Rearrange the furniture.
Make a list of things to do.
Think.
Ponder.
Water all the plants.
Sharpen all the pencils.
Look out the window.
Straighten everything in sight.
Count the snags in the carpet:
One, two, three, four...
We'll never get new carpet.
Think.
Ponder.
Recite the names of all the presidents, in order.
Who came after Jackson?
Look it up.
Martin Van Buren.
Maybe I could write a clerihew about every president.
But what would rhyme with "Van Buren?"
Martin Van Buren /
Was a man pure in /
Heart, but some things he neglected /
And he didn't get reelected.
That stinks, but what can you do with "Van Buren?"
And "Eisenhower"—what about that?
"Wise in power?"
"Dies in flower?"
Wait a minute —
Where did all these people come from?
And they're all coming towards me.
Time to get busy.
Well...
It's better than being bored.

By Degrees

M.L.S.
M.L.I.S.
M.A.L.S.
M.S.L.S.
(There may be others I don't know.)
Different combinations of letters
that all mean the same thing.

Does any other profession
have so many variations
on its basic credential?

So many ways to say:
"This is what you need
to do what we do.
If you've got this,
you're one of us."

Probably not,
and I'd like to think
it's because we are
a competent yet tolerant bunch —
even though we insist on a standard,
we're not all that fussy
about what we call it.

Come Live with Me
in the Library

Come live with me in the library,
And we'll sleep between the stacks.
We'll iron your dress in the old book press,
And we'll dine on vending snacks.

Come live with me in the library,
And our life will be so nice.
We'll read all night by a single light,
So we won't disturb the mice.

Come live with me in the library,
And our life will be complete.
We'll be safe and warm from winter's harm
By the laminator's heat.

Come live with me in the library,
And we'll thrive in wedded bliss.
We'll trade fond looks as we shelve the books—
Who could ask for more than this?

Elusive Lucy

Elusive Lucy reached her peak
At childhood games of hide-and-seek
And spends her time as an adult
In pursuit of the same result.

All calls to her go unreturned,
All invitations quickly spurned
Because, she says, she doesn't know
Where she will be, so she can't go.

Ostensibly, she is employed
And yet her desk is always void
Of any clue that Lucy was
At labor there, or what she does.

Attempts to reach her through the mail
Are guaranteed as well to fail
And postmen, pressed, will all confess
She's known as "Not at This Address."

Despite the rumors that persist
That she does not in fact exist,
Lucy does live — exclusively
To spend her time elusively.

For Men Only

Library men should wear a tie —
Though I don't know exactly why
Someone dictated long ago
That round our neck the noose should go.

Why did this genius, still unknown,
Apply this rule to males alone?
Perhaps he though we looked so wise
When roped and tethered by our ties?

But some I know refuse to wear
A tie at all. They just don't care
For silly rules— THEY never fret
About library etiquette.

Founding Father

Melvil Dewey was so clever:
Numbers followed by a dot.
Now today
In every way,
More than ever,
Dots are hot.

Just think of an IP address:
Numbers followed by a dot.
It works well
And it drew, Mel,
From your success,
Like as not.

Forty Years a Cataloger

Forty years a cataloger, she wonders
if anyone has matched that record,
in her state, at least,
but she doesn't know.
Nor does she know
how many thousands of books
she has cataloged in four decades,
though people sometimes ask —
more often now than before.
It never occurred to her
to keep a personal count.

But once in a while
she does gaze at the shelves
and considers how much of her work,
her life, is spread across there.
Each book is a payment of her time,
minutes drawn from her account.
Only she, of course, sees it that way;
no one else pays any mind
to how these books came to be
on the shelves and in the catalog.

It doesn't bother her.
Long ago she stopped worrying
about the thankless aspects of her job,
and how so many picture it
as the depressing enclave of drones.
In middle age she knew for certain
she had not made a mistake,
and brushed away youthful doubts.
Someone had to do this,
she was good at it, she liked it,
and that was enough.

When urged, she can reminisce
about the days of manual typewriters,
three-by-five cards, and endless filing.
Early computers, early computing.
Programs and routines from long ago
that at the time seemed so bold,
so innovative, but now seem quaint,
amusing in their debility.
She supposes her young colleagues
see her the same way:
the anachronism, the holdover.
She really doesn't care.
What do they know of time and change?

Recently, she has caught herself nodding off
a few times in front of her computer;
just for moments, but she wakes with a start
and quickly glances around.
She is bothered by these lapses,
but only a little;
she still gets the work out.
No great backlog betrays her age,
and if she loiters a bit longer
over books that interest her,
there's no harm in that.

Retirement stands outside her window,
a long-awaited blind date
with a sweet flower in his lapel.
He keeps checking his watch,
but she isn't ready for him, not just yet.
There are still books, records, corrections.
She can't just walk away from them.
Not today, and not tomorrow.
Maybe next year.
She's a cataloger,
she gets things done.

Home, Sweet Library

Years ago we had a librarian
who moved into the library —
to live, not to work,
although he did work here, too.
Darren was his name,
a likeable young fellow
who took his first job with us.
He didn't move in right away.
When we hired him,
he lived with his wife
in an apartment nearby.
Then one day they quarreled,
she threw him out,
and he had nowhere to go.
He moved into the library that night,
as we learned much later,
since Darren kept it a secret.
He kept his clothes and a few things
hidden in a rarely-opened closet.
Everything else he stashed
in the trunk of his car,
which he parked in different places
a few blocks from the library.
He didn't want to park the car
in the library lot overnight
and give a clue to his being there.
Darren would leave at closing time,
then come back after awhile,
making sure the custodians had left.
He slept in a sleeping bag
spread out on the carpet.
In the early morning, he rolled it up
and hid it carefully in the closet.
He sponge-bathed and shaved
with water from the men's room sink.

He cooked his meals in the staff lounge,
in the microwave, and dumped the remains
outside in the big trash bin.
He was careful about the lights,
leaving the visible ones off
when it grew dark outside.
There was no evidence he lived here.
Once in awhile one of us came in
while the library was closed
and we always found Darren here,
but he acted busy and told us
he was catching up on some work.
We never suspected anything.
Then one day someone got the notion
to clean out that rarely-opened closet.
Darren was out on the floor then
and knew nothing about it
until he saw his shirts and underwear
stacked on a table in the back.
He had no choice but to confess.
We knew he hadn't done any harm,
but of course there were rules
that didn't allow living in the library,
so Darren moved in with a friend.
Not too long after that,
he made up with his wife
and returned to their apartment.
They moved away a year later.
Darren got a job in another library.
We used to hear from him sometimes,
but not any more.
Distance can't help but reduce
the things people have in common.
Just the same, Darren's residence here
remains a running joke,
and we always wonder
if he'll do it again, somewhere else.

I'd Like You to Meet...

Our conservation librarians, **Rip Page** and his wife **Mindy**.
Our acquisitions librarian, **Will Order**.
Our director, **Dick Tate**.
Our secretary, **Arial Font**.
Our janitor, **Dusty Walls**.
Our fund raiser, **Buck Chase**.
Our head cataloger (he's retired military), **General Subdivision**.
Our shelving supervisor, **Miss Place**.
Our book processor, **Miss Label**.
Our readers' advisor, **Page Turner**.
Our circulation librarian, **Penny Fine**.
Our microcomputer repairman, **Chip Slaughter**.
Our interlibrary loan librarian, **Linda Farr**.
Our archivist, **Memo Provenance**.
Our federal depository librarian, **Sue Docker**.
Our literacy specialist, **Alf A. Betz**.
Our shelver, **Phil McCart**.
Our children's librarian, **Rita Story**.
Our young adult librarian, **Tina Angel**.
Our city manager, **Les Wages**.
Our binder, **Octavo Sheets**.

"I'm a Librarian"

The following are
the ten most frequent responses
when I answer,
"I'm a librarian"
to the question,
"What do you do for a living?"

1. So, I guess you like to read?
2. Do you have to go to school for that?
3. You don't *look* gay.
4. Can you make a living doing that?
5. I used to be a librarian. I worked in the library
   when I was in high school.
6. Tell me — what have they done with the card catalog?
7. I haven't been to the library in twenty years.
8. Not many men do that, do they?
9. That reminds me — I've got some old books in my garage
   that I need to give to the library.
10. Do you use a computer very much?

Incognito

I like to go to other libraries
where they don't know me,
to look and to learn,
but mostly to be just another patron;
where I can ask questions
instead of answering them
and see a library from the other side,
the only side that really matters.

It's enough to wander around
rediscovering things so familiar
I've forgotten them,
and seeing for the first time
clever little twists and touches
I can borrow and use.

Before I came to library work,
I never thought it a luxury
(a pleasure, but not a luxury)
to sit in a reading room with a book
as long as I liked, but now
it has the feel of something stolen,
yet no less sweet for the dash of guilt.

I said I don't answer questions.
I don't, but sometimes
I overhear the banter
between librarian and patron,
and I have to hold myself
from chiming in;
but even if I did,
I know they'd look at me
as some unwelcome know-it-all.

No, I've learned it's better
to keep quiet in the background
and leave them on their own.
Eavesdroppers are never recognized
as authorities, anyway.

It's in the Stars

To help you all cope,
Here's your horoscope,
The same if you're Taurus or Pisces:

Your library day
Will be quite okay
Except for the hourly crises.

It's Just Another Day

The reference desk is stacking up,
The bathrooms are all backing up,
I'm very close to cracking up,
It's just another day.

The telephones are all on hold,
The heat is out — it's getting cold,
I'm feeling very tired and old,
It's just another day.

My night relief just called in sick,
This patron is a lunatic,
I'll kill him if I don't leave quick,
It's just another day.

Somebody fell — they say they'll sue,
The heat's still out, I'm turning blue,
And my retirement's overdue,
It's just another day.

I've Got a Library PhD : A Song

This song is not intended as an insult to anyone holding a doctoral degree; rather, it is a good-natured poke at those few pretentious academics who are entirely lacking in practical experience. We've all known at least one!

I conceived this song as similar to those in the comic operas of Gilbert and Sullivan. Picture on stage a waspish, bespectacled man in a three-piece suit backed by a chorus of clones...

I've got a library PhD!
I've never worked in a libraree!
Still, you should be impressed, you see —
I've got a library PhD!

(Chorus)
He's got a library PhD!
He's never worked in a libraree!
Still, you should be impressed, you see —
He's got a library PhD!

I am a scholar through and through,
And did I mention my IQ?
Though my experience counts for naught,
I compensate by splendid thought.

Management books rest on my shelf;
I've even written some myself.
Theory I know from A to Z —
I've never worked in a libraree!

He's got a library PhD!
He's never worked in a libraree!
Still, you should be impressed, you see —
He's got a library PhD!

I know the latest buzzwords, too;
I've even tried to coin a few.
All my conclusions are oblique,
Phrased in the latest doublespeak.

I serve on panels, councils, boards;
I have a wall full of awards,
But if you search through my CV,
You won't find time in a libraree!

He's got a library PhD!
He's never worked in a libraree!
Still, you should be impressed, you see —
He's got a library PhD!

Students respect me as a sage,
Dean of the Information Age!
I think my students are terrific,
Just so their questions aren't specific.

Applicants come from near and far
Just to attend my seminar.
None of them know, despite my fee,
I've never worked in a libraree!

He's got a library PhD!
He's never worked in a libraree!
Still, you should be impressed, you see —
He's got a library PhD!

Though some insist that I'm a sham,
I shall continue as I am.
This is the perfect life for me —
Who wants to work in a libraree?

He's got a library PhD!
He's never worked in a libraree!
Still, you should be impressed, you see —
He's got a library PhD!

Let Us Wear White Coats

Let us wear white coats, as doctors do,
to show the serious nature of our profession.
Let our names be embroidered on the breast,
with the letters of our degrees following.

Let us adopt a demeanor of distracted gravity
and walk with a stride full of purpose.
Let every movement of hand and eye be confident,
decisive, yet economical in execution.

Let us impart our carefully guarded knowledge
in tones low and sonorous, pausing for effect.
Let us answer all questions with candor,
but never stray from our professional reticence.

Let us wear white coats, as doctors do—
come to think of it, in the better restaurants
so do waiters, even busboys.
Never mind!

Let us wear black robes, as judges do...

Libraria

We are citizens of Libraria,
that great country of outposts worldwide,
dispersed yet united.
Our many languages are one,
our goals diverse yet the same.
Spell our nationality
with a capital L:
Librarians.

Librarian Ghost

Oh, please won't you bury
Beneath the library
My body when I buy the farm.

I won't make a sound here,
I'll just hang around here,
And I won't do anyone harm.

And then my ambition
Can come to fruition:
To haunt the library awhile.

I won't be a bad ghost,
I'll just be a glad host
Who leaves everyone with a
    smile.

I'll float through the foyer
Of my old employer,
But I won't be overly scary.

I'll welcome all patrons,
From children to matrons,
To their newly-haunted library.

I'll swoop and I'll caper,
I'll fade like a vapor
And fill everyone with delight.

I'll be so endearing
As I am appearing
Throughout the library each
    night.

Old friends I'll be greeting,
New friends I'll be meeting.
I'll shake all their hands and I'll
    bow.

And soon all will hear it:
A jovial spirit
Resides in the library now.

The crowds will come swarming,
And I'll be so charming,
We'll soon be known
    throughout the nation.

Our fame will be growing —
We'll also be showing
A big rise in our circulation.

Now, some may be leery
Of ghosts who are cheery,
While others may just scoff and
    laugh;

But who else can boast
A librarian ghost
Is part of their permanent staff?

Librariangels,
Librariantagonists

"I have always imagined that Paradise will be a kind of library."
— Jorge Luis Borges

So...if Heaven will be a library,
wouldn't we librarians be running the place?
If so, being called "librarians" wouldn't be enough;
what about "librariangels?"

(Which leads me to the ghastly thought
that my director would be some kind of archangel.)
I suppose our pages would be cherubs.
I have visions of us all flying through the stacks,

Swooping to the lower shelves,
plucking books for our patrons
and tucking them inside our robes
(the books, not the patrons) for safe transit.

Sometimes an in-flight collision
would be inevitable, but not to worry —
there's no pain in Paradise.
A few scattered books, some ruffled wings.

"Sylvia never can make that turn around the 800's."
"Yeah, and Mark is sure slow on the takeoff
since he gained all that weight."
"Uh-huh. Well, I've put on a few myself."

At staff meetings we'd have no table
but simply float in a circle, munching on manna
while feigning concern about the agenda.
No, wait — in Heaven there would be NO staff meetings!

And all our patrons would be cheerful and kind,
our shelves in perfect order,
our computers always up,
with no waiting on the Web.

But how would Borges imagine Hell?
The anti-library? Replete with everyone
who ever worked against the ideals of librarydom?
Boy, we could fill that place up *fast!*

Just think: everlasting torment for all those
who sliced our budgets, berated our staff,
or lied about their lost library books.
They deserve a name, too: librariantagonists.

We'd put these misguided misanthropes to work
at all the tasks that have confounded us forever,
only we would make them ten, a hundred,
a thousand times worse.

Beneath a clock perpetually set
to five minutes before closing time,
Our librariantagonists would labor,
moaning for mercy to no avail,

Seeking the book that's never on the shelf,
suffering the verbal stones of abusive patrons,
searching for nonexistent MARC records
on ancient computers that constantly crash.

And as their pathetic wails drifted upward,
we librariangels would lean back in our recliners,
turn up the volume on our radios
and ponder what to have for lunch.

Borges may have had a point after all...

Library School Dropout

He still loves libraries.
He still visits them frequently.
But it's different now
when he's in a library.
Looking at the librarians,
they seem more distant,
not the same persons
as when he was on track
to become one of them.

Is graduate school always like this?
I bet not, in another program.
Those guys in the business school
go out and party every night
while I'm in the library
working on this stuff.
My eyes hurt, my head hurts.
Don't these professors understand
how much stress they're putting on us?
Every one of them acts like
hers is the only course we're taking.

He has a job now.
After he dropped out,
he wasn't sure what to do.
The big plan had gone bust,
and there was no Plan B.
What do you do, anyway,
with a degree in English,
no teaching credentials?
He read the classifieds
and got a job.
Proofreader, night shift.
Hourly wage. Punch a clock.

I can't do this.
I don't even understand it.
Everybody else in this class
has worked in a library
or works in a library now.
Everybody except ME.
They're talking over my head,
and the professor encourages it!
I have no idea what they're saying
most of the time...

He hates the job.
It's depressing.
A dingy typesetting plant
in the inner city.
All night long,
into the early morning hours,
marking copy with a red pencil,
looking for typographical errors,
head bent down under a lamp,
little human contact.
A few feet away, unmuffled,
the loud clatter of the linotypes
goes on and on and on.

It's not what I expected.
What does this have to do
with working in a library?
You never use most of this,
so why do they teach it?
Your real education is on the job —
everybody knows that.
I'm not getting this.
First big test is tomorrow.
What am I gonna do?

During the daytime,
he tries to sleep, but can't.
It's noisy outside his apartment.
Traffic comes and goes.
They mow the grounds.
The phone rings: salesmen, wrong numbers.
He goes to the libraries, sits there,
and thinks about what went wrong.

This isn't working out.
I made a mistake.
Bad career choice.
It's not for me.
My grades on those first tests were okay,
but I think I was just lucky.
I still don't think I understand it.
I wish there was someone
I could talk to.

And it does feel different in the libraries.
Not just the librarians; everything,
now that he knows for sure
he'll never work in a place like this.
Not that he feels like an outsider —
no, more than ever he has a sense
this is where he belongs;
he feels like a recruit
who abandoned his outfit.
Library school? It wasn't that bad;
was it, really? Confusing, yes,
but he should have stuck it out.
They all say it gets easier
after the first semester.

Well, I'm gonna do it. Today.
Withdraw. From the whole program.
They may try and talk me out of it,
but my mind's made up.
I can do something else.
I don't know what, but something.
Back to square one.

It came in the mail today.
The application.
Easier to do the second time.
They already have his scores,
transcripts, everything else.
Talking to advisors, he feels encouraged.
This time it'll work out.
Leave that rotten job,
concentrate on the courses,
get through.
It'll work out.

Lioness

Our middle school librarian
Is withered, mean, and old.
She's quite authoritarian,
Unsmiling, stern, and cold.

The youngsters shrink before her glare
And find her very scary:
A lioness who guards her lair,
The middle school library.

A few like her are with us yet,
But fewer would be better;
And crowds will cheer the day we get
Her resignation letter.

Musclebound Sadie

Musclebound Sadie, the library lady,
My lover, my sweet bride-to-be.
I'll never forget the day that we met
And she laid the law down to me.

While reading a book in the southeastern nook,
I sang out as I lingered there.
She told me be quiet — I said, "Make me, try it!"
And she yanked me out of my chair.

She gave me a headlock that tore off a dreadlock
And quickly, a full body slam.
I bounced off the floor, she did it once more.
I shouted, "Have mercy, please, ma'am!"

I was so enamored that my poor heart clamored
To know more of this Amazon.
So we started dating, no procrastinating —
In no time our romance was on.

One night as we nestled, she said that she wrestled;
In fact, she had once been a pro.
But she found that reading was more fun than bleeding,
Or even the Russian Death Blow.

And soon we shall marry here in the library,
Attended by pages and clerks.
I'll sit back in that chair and all day I shall stare
At Sadie, my love, while she works.

Quiet Consistency

She worked in this library thirty-eight years.
Just a girl, really, when she came here,
and to no one's knowledge ever sought another job.
Always in the background, never seeking attention,
but faithful to show up every day and do her work
with a quiet consistency that was mostly overlooked.

Oh, everyone liked and admired her, but in that way
you like and admire a good piece of furniture
because it is solid, durable, and unobtrusive.
People who had worked with her for years
didn't know the slightest thing about her personal life —
not that she ever talked about it.

I wonder if she ever got tired of the sameness,
so many indistinct days, through all those years?
Although I suppose when seen from her point of view,
she was the constant around which everything changed:
six directors, any number of come-and-go employees,
and all the usual mutations of the workplace over time.

So maybe she really was content to observe,
mostly in silence, just as she did her job.
When she retired, we had a party, of course,
gave her little gifts and a card we all signed,
and told her how much we envied her newfound freedom.
Still, it was a surprisingly somber occasion.

But she didn't cry at the party or later when she left;
in fact, no one could remember seeing her cry, ever.
When I think of her, I think of the cover of a book,
jacketless, boards and spine a nondescript drab color.
No one pays any attention to such a cover,
but it holds the book together quite dependably.

Reference Queen

Sweet Joanie is our Reference Queen,
The best darn one I've ever seen!
She fields all questions with acumen,
Her knowledge is near superhuman!
No subject is beyond her ken —
I've said before, I'll say again
She is the greatest of the great!
But I've begun to think of late
Although she is magnificent,
Some of our staff just might resent
Her expertise, her witty quips,
And on her desk, that jar marked "Tips."

Requiescat

Old catalogers never die.
They just get withdrawn.

The Thinker

As is his longtime preference,
Our Walter sits at Reference,
Motionless sometimes for hours
Summoning his mental powers.
Though these powers as yet falter,
This has not discouraged Walter,
Who is certain that his talents
Will emerge forth in the balance
And his genius long neglected
In the end will be respected.

Shelf-Destructive

Rest in peace, Prunella Furley,
Gone away from us too early.
Gone away your frowning face,
All for lack of shelving space.
Oh, how much those big books weighed!
Crammed in shelves that groaned and swayed,
Floor to ceiling, large and massive.
Your reaction was impassive:
Still you packed them ever tighter
And the shelves grew none the lighter.
Then one day you found yourself
Bending to the bottom shelf,
Grabbed a book and pulled with force,
But it wouldn't budge, of course,
So with unremitting ardor
Still you pulled it ever harder;
Though your struggle was protracted,
Finally it was extracted.
You fell backwards, you were floored.
"Victory is mine!" you roared—
All at once death came upon you
When a thousand books fell on you.
Yes, Prunella, thus you died:
Dead, alas, by bibliocide.

So They Claim

Our Serials Librarians
Are tactful, wise, and strong
Because, of course, they have to deal
With issues all day long.

Types

The **Acronymph**
is a young female librarian
who never speaks a full name
when an acronym will do.
She loves initial encounters.

The **PAC Rat**
can't tear himself away
from the online catalog.
He truly has a terminal problem.

The **Authority Control Freak**
will definitely remember your name —
and even change it.

The **Easy MARC**
accepts records as they are,
even when some changes
are indicated.
(Why bother?)

The **Serial Killer**
loves to cancels subscriptions.
Otherwise, he seems perfectly ordinary,
even nice.

Among the Jivaro Indians,
the **Shrunken Head Librarian**
was a position of great prestige.

The **Round Table Hopper**
loses interest in a hurry
and moves on to something else.

The **Photocopycat**
reproduces everything.
In science fiction circles,
she is also known as
The Duplicator.

The **Prepub Crawler**
takes great interest
in things yet to come.

The **Interlibrary Loan Shark**
uses strongarm tactics
to get materials returned.
Bring it back on time,
or she'll pay you a visit.

The **Webmaster of Library Science**
is a handy person to have around.
She can work with hypertext
and full text
in any context.

A stack supervisor (male)
who aspires to be a hip-shaking rock star
could be known as
Shelvis.
Which leads one to wonder:
could an interlibrary loan librarian (female)
who aspires to be a wildly-dressed singer
be known as
Share?

Virtual Librarian

I'm the virtual librarian: unseen, unheard, unknown,
Living in the bandwidth, ethereal, alone.
I'm neither male nor female, neither young nor old,
Unfettered by exhaustion, immune to heat or cold.

I'm the virtual librarian — you know me by my work:
Illuminating pathways through the electronic murk.
I've never looked upon you, nor have you looked at me,
Yet still we've met without the need of corporeity.

I'm the virtual librarian, appearing at your whim,
A tireless drone who'll serve your needs until the screen goes dim.
Anonymous and faceless, I'll gladly be your guide
And long before this day is through, a thousand more beside.

Would Anyone Care?

If we all walked off
From our jobs today,
Would anyone care
We'd all gone away?

Would anyone care
Beyond a few gripes
We'd all gone away,
We library types?

Would anyone care
If we didn't return?
We may never know,
We may never learn.

THE READING LIFE

Advice

Always carry a book.
It makes you feel and look
Informed and intellectual.

It gives the right effect,
And no one will suspect
You're dull or ineffectual.

Appearances

As with people,
So with books:
Often those with
Flashy looks
Offer little
Deep within,
To the reader's
Great chagrin;
While other books,
Although plain,
Bring the reader
Greater gain.
Story's moral?
Look inside
Books or people,
Then decide.

Batteries Not Required

A book doesn't need a power source —
Unless you count your brain, of course!

Each of Us Is a Book

Each of us is a book,
written as we live,
under constant revision.
Our content is never certain
from our appearance,
and though we try hard
to index our every line,
we overlook as much as we find,
leaving the question
of what is within us
largely a mystery,
even to ourselves.

Each moment of our lives
draws from the dual accounts
of that which is already written in us
and that which is being written.
Though we think we act
always as our own editor,
so often we merely provide
the blank pages for fresh copy
or proofs from the past for correction.
Some of us are so heavily marked,
in fact, that our original manuscript
may be unrecognizable.

We read each other, poorly,
hampered in comprehension
by our limited literacy
and myopic vision.
Most of us avoid
the complicated passages,
and we always reach
our separate conclusions
on the meaning and worth
of all we read.

We are each parts of a larger set,
though mismatched;
continuous in publication,
yet every one of us
is eventually weeded out,
leaving only a memory,
which in the end
is the only true book of all.

The Best Books

Though books read online
Are all well and fine,
Those held in the hand
Are in more demand.

For online books strain
The eyes and the brain,
And headaches ensue
From reading them, too.

But books that are bound
Have always been found
To comfort and please:
They're read with great ease.

So paper and ink
Will be here, I think
For centuries yet,
Lest anyone fret.

Book Jackets

With an odd combination of duties,
a book jacket is designed
to sell the book
and protect it;
a public relations specialist
who doubles as a bodyguard.

Favorite Books

Favorite books on a shelf,
unopened sometimes for years,
bring joy by their mere presence
and comfort in the knowledge
that familiar words await,
immutable on the printed page
as constellations stamped on the sky.

Fruit

Shelves full of books:
trees heavy with fruit,
ready to be picked,
always in season.

And the fruit
is always ripe,
never spoils,
And can be eaten over and over and over.

How-to

There's a how-to book
for almost everything,
except how to write
a how-to book.
How-to how-to,
which sounds like an island
in the South Pacific,
but isn't such a book needed?
Wouldn't a lot of people
write a how-to book
if only they knew how to?
And if one of those writers
who writes how-to books
knows how to write
a how-to book
about how to write
a how-to book,
why doesn't he write it?
Is he afraid
he might create
too much competition?

Illiteracy

The illiterate life
Is like losing your fingers:
Long after the trauma
The damage still lingers;
Most things in the world
Are beyond your touch
And try as you might,
You just can't grasp much.

In Memory Of

Little tombstones, I used to call them,
those "In Memory Of" bookplates.
That was when I was much younger,
before I began to lose friends and family.
Now I notice the plates for what they are,
a poignant tribute of the best sort,
a badge of love stuck on the breast
of one of humankind's finest achievements
and our closest mimicry of the eternal:
a book.

They are scattered throughout our collection.
I never know when, by random selection,
I will open a book as I open a door
and be greeted by the name of someone
loved enough to be remembered
through the gift of a book to strangers.
Most of the names are long forgotten,
many of the books are tattered, archaic,
but I never weed a book
with a memorial plate — never.

In the Lingering Shadow of Sorrow

In the lingering shadow of sorrow,
a book is a steadfast friend
who keeps a silent vigil
within reach of the bereaved,
faithful to respond as needed,
yet as willing to remain mute
in solemn deference.

The Last Word Read

Few of us remember the first word we read,
yet there was one, as there was a first word spoken,
and one day we shall read our last word,
though we will probably not know it at the time.
I suspect for most of us the last word read
will be something undistinguished:
part of a label on a medicine bottle,
a fragment of a magazine ad,
a doctor's name stitched on his jacket.
Not many of us will suddenly drop dead
after reading the last word of *War and Peace.*
Some, from failing eyesight, read their last word
long before their demise, but even they
never know which elusive characters
they will see last in the waning light.
I would like to choose the last word I read,
but of course this is the sort of detail
one forgets in the confusion of dying.
Still, after a lifetime of loving to read,
it would be nice to conclude the flow
with a word of one's own choice.
More likely I will die in the library
after reading some meaningless report
and, just before I fade to black,
my eyes will see the sign marked "Exit."

Lower Level

We styled our basement by the book:
We knew exactly where to look
To find the right decor and plan.
And where was this? None other than
The standard on which all insist:
"The New York Times Best Cellar List."

Makeover

I wish there was a bindery
For people, as for books,
Where we could go for full repairs
To renovate our looks:

A brand-new outer covering,
A straight and strong new spine.
We'd still be old and worn within,
But outside, we'd look fine!

Mind Less

Though reading books expands the mind,
(I truly think it does)
His reading leaves his mind, I find,
Much smaller than it was.
It's not that he is not well-read,
Which no one would assume —
His mind instead has fled his head
To give his ego room!

Murder Mystery : A Poetic Synopsis

Classic story:
Murder, gory.
Suspects, varied.
Gumshoe, harried.
False diversions.
Strange excursions.
Romance sizzles.
Romance fizzles.

Danger lurking.
Gumshoe working.
Clues have dwindled.
Love rekindled.
Revelation.
Confrontation.
Climax, action.
Satisfaction.

Non-fiction

I've always been bothered by "non-fiction."
Not the books, but the term.
It implies that fiction is the norm;
hence, anything else is a variant:
NON-fiction.

Following this logic,
a woman is a non-man,
an adult is a non-child,
and so on.

And if fiction is the norm,
doesn't that mean we humans
are essentially liars
and anything written
that isn't a lie
must be noted as such?

Instead of "non-fiction,"
I'd like an alternative term.
I just haven't thought of a good one yet.
Apparently no one else has, either.
That must be why
we're still using "non-fiction."

I'll come up with something better.
In the meantime,
I'm still bothered by it,
and that's a non-lie.

Old Cookbooks

Old cookbooks: the stains tell stories.
A cookbook is a tool, after all,
and belongs in the kitchen.
Who minds a few stains on the pages?
Not me. I'm proud of our collection,
shelf after shelf, and prouder still
that the books circulate so freely.
The new ones are nice, pages slick,
filled with enchanting photographs
of foods so bright and lovely
they seem to have been made by fairies—
edible jewels that glisten in their perfection.

But I really like the old cookbooks better;
worn and weathered, they prove their service
by their battered appearance and the stains
they wear upon their pages.
Many have no photos at all,
or simply dull gray halftones
that do little to entice the palate,
and their outdated typefaces
present recipes in no-nonsense prose,
brief and businesslike.
These are manuals for busy homemakers.
They don't waste time on frills.

The stains do tell stories;
you have to use your imagination, of course,
to find a story behind the stain,
but that's not so hard.
Take this book: published in 1948,
mended a dozen times, still on our shelf.
(I won't let anyone weed it.)
Match the stains to the recipes
and think of someone decades ago
with this book spread open
on her kitchen counter,
trying out a new dish.

Spaghetti Bolognese — see the stains,
faded to pink after all these years?
The book says it's best
when served with garlic toast,
and our mystery chef dutifully prepared some,
as these yellowish stains prove.
And perhaps later that evening,
her happy family sat down
to a dinner that was new and exciting
in a less complicated time
when croissants and cappuccino
weren't sold in convenience stores.

And this recipe for brownies:
the cocoa stains all over the page
tell me a child was involved,
most likely a little girl
cooking with her mother.
Smudge after smudge of sweet brown goo,
each one the mark of a tiny finger
returning to check the instructions.
But here, a single amber stain
stands out among the chocolate;
maybe an egg? No, I think instead
it was a teardrop — the brownies may have burned.

Our Type

If Gutenberg
Had lost his zest,
Both he and we
Would be de-pressed.

Patterns

Most of us, when we die,
leave behind our memory
in patterns on paper, tapes, and disks.
A photograph may be reduced to dots,
yet from a distance it holds our image.
Though we are not the dots,
are we any more the image?
Any medium, for a given moment,
can capture what we were —
no, what we seemed to be,
but it is never us, only a pattern.
We dismiss photos as light and shadow,
portraits as streaks of color,
but what we see of our world
and declare as reality
are nothing more than patterns
upon our retina.

And our libraries gather patterns,
the memories and record of humanity
reduced to patterns of ink,
dots, oxide, pits, lands, and others;
for this is still all we have,
the best we know.
Though we are clever to create new patterns,
they are never the thing itself
and never will be;
so we measure their worth
as they convince in illusion.
The ancients kept the memory of their dead
and the secrets of their cultures
in tales told by holy men.
Today we keep our memories and secrets
in patterns, in libraries,
and each of us is a shaman
to ourself and one another.

Reading While the Rain Falls

Reading while the rain falls—
Could anything be better?
Outside it's getting wetter,
And although duty calls,
My inner child keeps pleading
To let me keep on reading,
reading, reading, reading,
reading while the rain falls.

Screened Out

It's nice to read from
    A computer screen;
Get what I need from
    A computer screen;
So much indeed from
    A computer screen;
But for a longer look,
I much prefer a book.

They Also Serve

They also serve who stand and wait,
But books that never circulate
Will find that weeding is their fate.

Weading

The books I try to weed
I browse through and I read,
And hours soon are gone,
While nothing gets withdrawn.

OUR PATRONS, OURSELVES

Another Saturday Morning

Another Saturday morning in the public library.
People come, people leave.
It's a different crowd than weekday mornings.
Younger, busier, more in a hurry.
No one stays very long.
It's Saturday morning, after all.
So many things to do, so many places to go.
The library is only one place on their list.
One stop on a frenetic path.
There are also soccer games, shopping.
Endless errands, urgent and routine.
Start early. Stop by the library.
And go on, keep going on.

A Curse and a Blessing

May patrons who borrow
And bring books back when late
Find great woe and sorrow
Forever their fate.

May patrons who borrow
And bring books back when due
With every tomorrow
Good fortune accrue.

Closed

Ten minutes after closing,
I see them from my office window
as they walk briskly up to the front door
and pull on it to no avail, thumpthump.
We're closed, but they didn't know it,
and they stand there a moment frustrated
as they scan the sign and talk to one another.
They can't see me, I can't hear them.

I watch them like an uncaptioned silent movie,
getting clues from their shrugs and nods.
I've seen this scene many times before,
with different actors, but it always plays the same.
And I always wonder:
Did they rush to get here?
Did they come from far away?
And what did they need…

After a moment they turn and leave,
disappointed but resigned —
(I should have called /
you should have called!)
Alone or in pairs, they return to their cars,
not so briskly now, but with that walk,
that strange intermittent stride
of those who have to change their plans.

Years ago, I might well have let them in,
just for a few minutes, maybe longer.
Not now, though, unless I know them,
but these latecomers are always strangers.
Times have changed.
Still, I share their disappointment
and whisper to their retreating forms,
I'm sorry, please come back when we're open.

Genealogy

So many patrons
interested in genealogy —
where do they all come from?
Actually,
I guess that's what *they* want to know.

Jim's Mail

I never knew Jim's last name
until he started getting his mail here,
but that's a story by itself.
He was one of those drifters
who come down from the north
in the winter seeking warmth
and a safe place to spend their days.
They find both in our library,
and from October to April
we play host to a rotating cast of them;
most move on after a few days,
maybe a week. None ever stayed longer
until Jim came along.

He was different from the others.
Oh, he was just as disheveled
and always needed a bath,
but he did keep his hair and beard combed
and even trimmed, more or less,
with a pair of old kitchen scissors.
He kept those scissors
and everything else he owned
in that greasy canvas backpack
he lugged around everywhere.
Looking at Jim, you knew right away
he'd been on the road for years,
but he weathered it better than most.

The main difference with Jim, though,
was in his personality, not his appearance.
He didn't show the usual litany of emotions
we see in most of his fellow travelers:
the undercurrent of anger,
the borderline lunacy
(in some, not borderline at all),
the overwhelming sense of futility.
Jim was always lucid, always pleasant,
and never seemed to question his circumstances
or even be bothered by them;
if he was troubled, he never told us
and he hid it well.

From the day he showed up,
he called me "Captain."
Maybe it was because I was the director;
more likely because he couldn't remember names.
One morning I was surveying the floor,
pondering some minor problem,
when a husky voice near my elbow asked,
"Looks pretty serious, huh, Captain?"
I looked down and there was Jim,
seated in an overstuffed chair, reading *Newsweek*,
and grinning at me so disarmingly
I grinned back; we ended up talking
fifteen minutes or more.

From then on, we were friends.
Jim arrived most mornings
right after the library opened, and stayed
until we closed or it got dark.
When I asked him where he stayed at night,
he was vague; he said he had a place
near the library, but wouldn't talk about it.
Somebody said he lived in a grove of trees
near the old railroad tracks, but nobody really knew.
During the day, he moved from chair to chair,
reading magazines and newspapers.
Sometimes he went outside in the sun
to sit on the bench and watch the birds.

Jim and I chatted every day,
often only a minute or two,
but I always felt better afterward.
He had a cheerful calm about him
that seemed to defuse stress in others;
and he was no addle-brained vagrant —
years of hanging out in libraries,
reading all day, had broadened his knowledge
and built his vocabulary.
Most of our discussions were better
than those I've had with self-styled scholars,
and Jim had none of the smugness or arrogance
I've found in so many of those people.

But even as we talked,
I never learned much about him —
not even his last name, at that point.
I gave him some of my old clothes,
although I was taller and heavier.
He wore them proudly: belts cinched up
around baggy trousers, shirtsleeves rolled up
to expose his bony wrists.
Later, I found a few small jobs for him
around the library; cleaning, mostly,
and paid him out of my pocket.
He was as grateful for those few dollars
as if he'd been a high-paid consultant.

One day we got a letter at the library
addressed to a "James Rackowski."
Nobody by that name was on our staff,
and we puzzled over who it could be;
then I thought of Jim, his daily presence,
and I took the letter to him.
Yes, he said, it was his;
he didn't think we would mind
if he used our address for his mail,
since he really couldn't get delivery
at his residence — was it okay?
I thought for a moment, and said
I didn't suppose it did any harm.

And the mail kept coming.
Not much, maybe one letter a week,
usually handwritten ones postmarked in Michigan,
a place I'd never heard Jim mention.
He never talked about those letters,
just thanked me as I brought them,
and I didn't ask any questions.
Spring came, and around mid–April
we didn't see Jim any more.
He never told us he was leaving —
one day he just wasn't there.
His mail, though, kept coming,
and I saved it in a drawer in my desk.

It's still coming, and every day I wonder
where Jim is and what he's doing.
Some of our staff have speculated
he's in jail or even dead —
I don't think so. We knew he'd leave
come springtime, and it's just as likely
he'll be back when it gets cold up north.
Anyway, I think he will.
I've got those letters in my drawer
waiting for him, all arranged
in the order they arrived.
One of these mornings we'll open up
and he'll be back.

Just Let Me Tarry

Just let me tarry
At the library
Before I must leave it behind.

I've found so much pleasure
And infinite treasure
Discovering things of the mind.

Just let me tarry
At the library
A moment before I depart.

I've so much to learn here
And so I'll return here
Discovering things of the heart.

nothing new

book so late
past the date
overdue
lost it too
tale of woe
we all know
every word
we have heard
nothing new
boo hoo hoo

One, Two, Three, Four

Have you noticed?
People come to the library
singly,
in pairs,
seldom in threes,
even less in fours,
and if more than four,
it's always an organized group:
a class, a meeting,
or some such,
which doesn't count
as a true drop-in visit.

Another thing:
the larger the group,
the less serious its purpose.
Pairs are never
as motivated
as singles,
while threes and fours
are downright frivolous,
and large groups
are hopeless.
(Have you ever known a class
that *really* paid attention?)

No, serious library users always come alone.
Single.
Solo.
Stag.
Someone should study this.
Someone probably has.
Somewhere, there's a dissertation
no one has ever read,
or ever will,
entitled something like:
The Inverse Benefit of Multiplicity
on the Cognitive Aspects of Library Visitation.

We have one of those patron counters
at our library entrance,
and if two or more people
enter abreast
it counts them as one.
I'm bothered by this—
not so much
by the uncounted patrons,
but because
that single count
gives too much credit
to the plurals.

Yes, I know
those patrons counters
only show totals,
but it's the thought
that troubles me.
There should be a way
to handle this,
to assign points
on a descending scale
based on the size of the group,
while making exceptions
for Siamese twins.

Overdue Notices with Style(s)

Do your patrons ignore your overdue notices?
Maybe they'd pay attention if you sent them
a notice in a style that is more appealing to
them...

Sentimental:

We've counted the moments
Since you've been away.
Our hearts fill with longing
To see you today,
And much as we miss you,
Still greater's our yearning
Our books will be with you
When you are returning.

Country and Western:

Time's drifted by,
The candle's burned,
But still them books
You ain't returned.
So search the trailer
And search the truck;
Bring 'em on back
And save a buck.

Hip-hop:

Yo! That book
You know you took
It's big-time late
So don't hesitate
Betta bring it back
Or you gonna pay us, Jack!

Blues:

Our computer's so slow
It's like draggin' a chain.
There's a hole in our roof,
And it's startin' to rain.
But those ain't the reasons
We been singin' the blues—
It's 'cause you're hangin' on
To all them overdues!
We got the blues, baby,
The blues from overdues.
Ain't but one thing that can cure 'em —
Bring those books back, don't refuse.

On Second Thought

Kids and libraries!
A match made in heaven.
Well…maybe…perhaps…
If they're over seven.

Kids and libraries!
The pairing brings joy.
Well…maybe…perhaps…
Have you met that new boy?

Kids and libraries!
The perfect career.
Well…maybe…perhaps…
Somewhere else besides here.

PPHOF

In our library, in the back
We have a pleasant little room.
Where we can rest and have a snack
And chase away the workday gloom.

And in one corner, on the wall
Inside a wooden-framed display,
Are faces known to one and all;
We put a new one in today.

But these aren't photos of our crew,
Our board, or gracious benefactors,
Or families, or friends we knew,
Or famous actresses and actors.

No, these aren't people that we love,
But lengthy captions by each name
Describe in detail members of
Our Problem Patron Hall of Fame.

Recommended Reading

She used to adore those mysteries,
But no longer finds them mysterious;

She used to adore those histories,
But no longer thinks they are serious;

She used to adore those romances,
But no longer feels sentimental;

So these days she just takes her chances—
My suggestions are quite incidental.

Reference Interview : A Poetic Dialogue

Young Patron:
> I think need some kind of book.

Librarian:
> For what exactly do you look?

Young Patron:
> You know, a book about a guy.

Librarian:
> Can you recall his name? (Please try.)

Young Patron:
> Uh, I don't know. I think he's dead.

Librarian:
> Do you know what he did, instead?

Young Patron:
> I think he did a lot of stuff.

Librarian:
> That really isn't quite enough...

Young Patron:
> He did some stuff— in history.

Librarian:
> (*That* makes it less a mystery!)

Young Patron:
> And if I heard his name, I'd know.

Librarian:
> You have to write a paper, though?

Young Patron:
> Yeah, it's due tomorrow morning.

Librarian:
> You had so little advance warning?

Young Patron:
> It was assigned a month ago...

Librarian:
> It's eight p.m. We close, you know —

Young Patron:
> At nine, I know, that's why I'm here.

Librarian:
> (And I chose *this* as my career?)

The Saddest Moment

The saddest moment of my library career
came years ago, when I was director
of a college library in a small city
full of shade trees and softly sloping hills;
a pleasant place, and of the library,
the worst that could be said was
the days were mostly predictable,
and some don't think that's a bad thing at all.

I heard one day of a terrible accident,
a car wreck, in front of the campus.
One of our students was killed, a girl,
nineteen years old, a freshman.
Her picture was in the newspaper the next day,
a radiant face with a smile full of hope,
and I grieved a minute for her, and that hope.

A few days later, a middle-aged woman
came to the library with an armful of our books.
She was the girl's mother, she explained,
and these books had been in the car
with her daughter during the accident;
she apologized if they were late.
Soft-spoken and sincere, her voice quavered
despite her best efforts to be calm.

For a few painful seconds, I couldn't answer her;
then I thanked her as I insisted
there was no need to apologize,
and I was so sorry for her loss.
I watched her back as she left the library
and walked alone through throngs of students
who chatted and laughed as her daughter did
only a few short days ago.

I didn't know the girl,
but I pictured her in the library,
smiling, checking out these books,
never knowing she wouldn't live to return them.
As I gathered the books off the counter,
I noticed on a couple of them
a few tiny drops of dried blood.

The Roving Random Reader

The Roving Random Reader —
Beware, my friend, and heed her!
Between the shelves she's sprinting
With eyes agape and glinting.

The Roving Random Reader —
Oh, don't try to impede her!
She darts about with vigor
As if fired by a trigger.

The Roving Random Reader —
Hold back, and don't precede her!
She grabs with wild abandon
Each book she puts her hand on.

The Roving Random Reader —
She's danger, but we need her!
Despite our consternation,
She boosts our circulation!

Snippy Patrons

Snippy patrons snip and snipe,
Finding glee in every gripe,
Hoarding anger as if gold,
Nursing grudges grown so old,
Spewing spite that never ends.
Snippy patrons have few friends

Things Left Behind

People leave things behind in the library.
Some things are left by accident:
gloves, purses, backpacks, keys.
Other things are left on purpose:
teenagers, business cards, religious tracts,
graffiti in the restrooms.
Things left by accident are usually retrieved,
but sometimes they remain abandoned
to become wards of the library.
After awhile in Lost and Found,
usually some corner of the circulation desk,
the fate of these orphans must be decided.
Some libraries have policies. Most don't.
So the calculator or tablet may be drafted
into the library workforce,
while the random piece of clothing
("That's a *beautiful* scarf!")
may be adopted by a staff member.
Everything else left by accident is mostly discarded,
as are many things left on purpose,
except teenagers, who get a ride home,
and graffiti, which is scrubbed or painted.
Things discarded end up in the landfill,
which, besides the library,
is the other great collective memory of our time.

THE WRITING LIFE

Library Bard

Do you yearn to be
A library bard?
Well, take it from me,
It's not very hard:

Read poetry first
In volumes galore,
The best and the worst.
When done, read some more;

Read just for enjoyment;
Then after awhile
Observe the employment
Of words, voice, and style;

(For never a crafter
Who values his trade
Pursues a skill after
His craftwork is made);

Learn meter and rhyme —
Some say they're passé,
But they've stood through time
And still stand today;

Ply your profession
For twenty-five years;
Note with discretion
The laughter and tears;

Then scrawl out a line
Direct from the heart,
Revise and refine,
And you've made a start.

To "Anonymous"

You're one yet all
Whom none recall,
Unpaid, unsung, unknown.

Of all who write,
There's none we cite
As much as you alone.

When we don't know
Who wrote it so
Or maybe only said it,

We give to you
The author's due:
The byline and the credit.

Missing the Point

All poetry with a light touch
Is never valued half as much
As that within a darker vein
That deals with anger, grief or pain.

It seems all those who would anoint
Themselves as critics miss the point:
In verse, as life, sheer happiness
Is to be valued more, not less.

These critics seem to speak as one:
Averse to verse that's just for fun,
While we who write light verse and such
Find we don't care for critics much.

It's clear they haven't met our muse,
But ignorance is no excuse.
(And need I mention that a critic
Is by nature parasitic?)

And so I write my poems to please
The denizens of libraries,
Who have no grudge they need to nurse
Against the merits of light verse.

Trashy Writing

I'm compiling a coffee table book.
It's in two parts.
The first part is photographs
of the world's finest landfills.
The second part is a collection
of the world's finest fiction.
I'm going to call the book
Great Litter: A Tour and Great Literature.

Writers' Gallery

*An eclectic collection of poetic sketches
of writers past and present*

Edward Albee

Critics are in awe of you.
All I ever saw of you
Seemed so shallow and contrived.
Still, through all these years you've thrived:
Lots of screaming confrontations
And eccentric situations.

Louisa May Alcott

Little Women is delightful,
Sensitive, warm, and insightful.
Children still should read and know
Of Amy, Beth, Meg, and Jo.

Stephen Ambrose

Reading history can be a chore,
But your books are never a bore.
Keep them coming, keep us learning,
And to you we'll keep returning.

Jane Austen

Heroines extraordinary,
Sometimes the epistolary,
Paths to conjugality,
Questions of morality,
Ever full of sentiment,
Talent that is evident.

L. Frank Baum

If ever an author I'd like to thank,
I'd like to thank, to thank you, Frank,
Because, because, because, because, because —
Because, my friend, you gave us Oz!

Lord Byron

I don't think you'd rank as high
If you'd been an ugly guy.

Agatha Christie

Mysteries with zest and flair,
Wit, suspense — it's all in there;
And as most detectives go,
You can't beat Hercule Poirot.

Charles Dickens

Characters of your creation:
They comprise a Dickens nation!
Pickwick, Scrooge, Uriah Heep
Make us laugh and make us weep;
Oliver, David, Little Nell,
And many more than we can tell,
Vivid now as they were then,
Offspring of your wondrous pen.

George Eliot

Silas Marner: underrated!
Mary Ann, I've always hated
That you had to write as "he"
When you really were a "she."

T.S. Eliot

Left the States, became a Briton.
I'm not fond of much you've written.
Some have called your verse the sweetest.
I myself think you're elitist.
Some would say J. Alfred's song
And your cat poems prove me wrong;
Still, I'm vexed by the profusion
Of your erudite allusion.

William Faulkner

Complex books that roam and sprawl —
Difficult, but all in all,
Something deep is running through them,
Scholars still are coming to them.

Robert Frost

I write poems — you're a *poet*.
There's a difference, and I know it.
Master of poetic tools,
Verses crafted fine as jewels,
Honors garnered by the score —
Pulitzer Prizes, you won four.

Bret Harte

Two short stories not forgotten;
Everything else, pretty rotten.

Ernest Hemingway

Macho drinking, macho thinking,
Macho fighting, macho writing.
You've influenced generations
With your macho inclinations.
Prose so lean and clean and tight,
Papa, you know how to write.

Jack Kerouac

Not a beatnik, you insisted;
But the image has persisted.
On the Road is still a trip,
You're the hippest of the hip.

Stephen King

How can someone so prolific
Be consistently horrific?
One more thing I can't explain —
All this from a guy from Maine?
Most agree upon one thing:
Horror fiction — you're the King.

Rod McKuen

Does anyone remember you,
And is there any reason to?

Herman Melville

Everybody knows the tale
Of Ahab and the great white whale.
Fewer know or have been told
When it came out, it hardly sold.

James A. Michener

Tales of history are your strength,
All in books of uncommon length,
Well-researched and in a style
Clear, concise, and worth our while.

Arthur Miller

Arthur, Arthur, I'm confessing
I find all your plays depressing.
If my life were like your people,
I'd jump off the nearest steeple.

Margaret Mitchell

Just one book was all you did,
(Not counting that one as a kid)
But your tale of Miss O'Hara,
Ashley, Rhett, and home, sweet Tara
Is sufficient, just the same,
To put "legend" by your name.

Joyce Carol Oates

Such an *oeuvre* you've created —
Still you're writing unabated,
Balancing the pedagogic
With your novels psychologic.

Dorothy Parker

Wit and wisdom most sardonic,
Wry and dry as gin and tonic.

Robert B. Parker

Here's to your Beantown private eye,
A tough but tender kind of guy,
A gourmet cook who quotes Shakespeare —
Spenser, he's the man, it's clear.

Edgar Allan Poe

Father of the form detective,
And your poems are so affective.
Tales of horror so macabre,
Tell-tale hearts will skip and throb.
Literary critic, too;
Man of many talents, you
Passed away at just twoscore:
Such a genius, nevermore.

Marcel Proust

À la Recherche du Temps Perdu.
From this alone, the world knows you.
The great *Remembrance of Things Past.*
From this alone, your name will last.

J.D. Salinger

Catcher in the Rye is great,
But how long we had to wait
For the rest, which isn't much.
Only once, that magic touch.

Dr. Seuss

Children flock to your creations,
Zany verse and illustrations.
No one else can draw like you:
Lorax, Horton and the Who,
Cat in the Hat, Grinch, and Yertle
From your pen and brush so fertile.
I, too, think you're pretty nifty
(I'm no kid — I'm over fifty.)

William Shakespeare

No one ever will approach you.
Not one reason to reproach you.
Centuries have passed and still
None have been your equal, Bill.
Every line and every phrase —
Ages pass, the magic stays.

Danielle Steel

Novels, novels, so romantic,
Written at a pace so frantic.
Women rich and glamorous,
Wrapped in plots so amorous.
Critics shun the tales you're telling,
By the millions you keep selling.

Robert Louis Stevenson

A Child's Garden brings a smile, and
Who can resist *Treasure Island*,
Dr. Jekyll and Mr. Hyde,
Kidnapped, Black Arrow, and *Ebb Tide?*

Leo Tolstoy

War and Peace, the critics state,
Is the greatest of the great;
Of all novels, none exceeds it.
(How come no one ever reads it?)

Mark Twain

Far beyond the Gilded Age,
You're enduring as a sage.
Sometimes cynical and spiteful,
Always witty and delightful.
Pudd'nhead is oh-so-clever,
Huck and Tom will live forever.

Walt Whitman

Modern verse? We've known for long
How it sprang from Whitman's *Song,*
Leaves of Grass, and others, too.
Walt, we owe a debt to you.

TOOLS OF THE TRADE

Down Time

Computers *do* give us
more leisure time.
Before computers,
when the power went out,
we'd light candles
and continue working.
Now, we still light candles
when the power goes out,
but we just sit around
until it comes back.

E-mail Junkies

E-mail junkies! Their addiction
Rules them like a dread affliction.
All their time is spent in sending
Silly e-mails neverending.

E-mail junkies! Male or female,
Day or night, they're sending e-mail,
Wasting bandwidth and resources
With their flood of vain discourses.

E-mail junkies! It's ironic
They adore mail electronic.
Most would never write a letter,
Yet somehow e-mail is better.

E-mail junkies! I've suspected
There are more than we've detected.
If you're mailing unrestricted,
Maybe you, too, are addicted!

The Ex-Files

When I started out
(And that's been awhile)
With card catalogs,
My job was to file.

I'd file them in drawers,
Those three-by-five cards.
It wasn't that bad,
Or without rewards.

By author, by title,
By subject as well.
I may have misfiled some —
It's too late to tell.

It

In every sight, every sound,
every word that is written,
every line that is read,
every byte that leaps across the bandwidth,
is both the essence and the totality
of that great collective *it*
that eludes us even as it engulfs us.

We call it by many names,
all of them insufficient;
we seek to capture it in many ways,
all of them inadequate.
In innocent vanity we think we can control it,
but we merely mimic what we cannot create.
Sea water in a bottle is not the ocean.

Listservs

Smoke signals
on the cyberplains
to the scattered tribes.

Listservs II

You're in Boston.
I'm in Dallas.
The rest of us
are spread across the nation,
even the world,
like beads torn from a necklace
and flung to the sky,
landing in a thousand random places,
yet reconnected, the same necklace,
on an invisible magic string.

Memory Lane

If you can remember
When these were required
To run a library,
It's time you retired!

electric styluses

carbon paper

manual typewriters

library catalogs on microfiche

library catalogs on printouts

keypunch machines

dictating machines

calculating machines (*not* calculators)

mimeograph machines

black rotary telephones with straight cords

film loop projectors

phonographs in carrying cases

78 rpm phonograph records

classified ads in the local newspaper
under the heading "Help Wanted, Female"

Old Computers

Like children with progeria,
you grow old so quickly:
middle-aged at two years,
elderly at four, and beyond that
mired in senescence, doddering, feeble,
relegated to trivial tasks
or turned out altogether,
abandoned without ceremony
for others who are younger, faster,
and more attuned to the times.
All too soon no one wants you.

Outage

When the network goes down,
net work goes down.

Outsourcing

This whole trend to outsourced service
Makes me insecure and nervous;
Cataloging, acquisitions—
Now I'm having strong suspicions
What our next outsource will be:
Are they going to outsource *me?*

Shelf Logic

We shelve books horizontal
So when we face them frontal
And take one from the shelf,
It comes out by itself.

Books stacked in columns high
Will save much space thereby,
But if one book's withdrawn,
The column's down and gone.

So we shelve side to side,
A method true and tried.
But I confess a liking
For columns. (Much more striking.)

Technical Manuals

How many unhappy hours have I spent
poring over these in extreme anguish?
Online, too—even worse
and not as well organized.
("Well" being a relative term.)
The demonic potential of words
is never more clear than here;
these manuals are the Antipoetry
of our culture, with their convoluted phrases,
maddeningly ambiguous definitions,
and endless cross-references.
Yet is there greater relief
than that which comes
when the directions are followed
and they actually *work?*

Traffic Jam

Back on the Web, and here I am,
Stuck in a bandwidth traffic jam.

It's just the same as in a car:
In traffic jams, you don't go far.

The traffic slows down to a crawl,
But mostly doesn't move at all.

Who knows what sort of data wreck
Has caused this latest bottleneck?

All morning long, or pretty near,
I've wasted my time sitting here.

I'd leave, but soon as I would go,
The traffic would begin to flow,

So I'll continue sitting here
Until the traffic starts to clear.

Web Tide

Our Internet access,
Despite all we've tried,
Goes out twice a day,
The same as the tide.

Some blame our technician,
Whom I don't impugn.
Instead, I'm convinced
It's caused by the moon.